MANAGING
STUDENT BEHAVIOR

For All Levels

JIM SHAULIS

Managing Student Behavior

ISBN: 978-0-9891240-0-3

Library of Congress Control Number: 2013908213

Jim Shaulis Publishing
Florida, USA

This book is dedicated to all teachers who care about their students and take pride in their work. Thank you for your endless hours and your professionalism.

Acknowledgments

Thanks to Richard Steinman, my former training partner, and my wife, Ruth Shaulis, a creative teacher, for their encouragement and suggestions.

Also, my appreciation goes to Sharen Lewis, an outstanding teacher, for her expert feedback.

The self-publishing of this book was made easy due to the direction and advice of the folks at Jera Publishing. Thank you, Kimberly, Jason, Stephanie, and Ryan.

jimshaulisbooks.com

<u>Managing Student Behavior for All Levels</u> is an excellent teacher resource. Using the presented tips and strategies will definitely strengthen your management skills. To get even more benefit, try using it as a book study in which you and a few colleagues get together for discussions and sharing. Everything you need is free on the above website.

Also on the website are free downloads of hand signal posters, self-reflection forms, and many other useful items.

Foreword

Classroom management refers to all of the things that a teacher does to organize students, space, time, and materials so that student learning can take place (Wong, & Wong, 2009, p. 83).

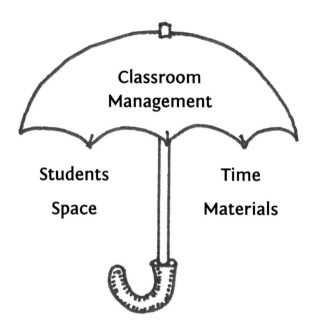

Although space, time, and materials are mentioned in this book, Managing Student Behavior is the main topic.

Every tip is based on the "tried and true." If delivered with consistency, these tips will make a positive impact on your classroom management.

> **The best way to eliminate job stress as a teacher is to take the time up front to hone your management skills and hold yourself to a high standard regarding their implementation and follow-through.**

Dedicated teachers are busy people, and their time is valuable. With that in mind, this book has been written in a concise format.

Contents

Introduction

As teachers, we have always known that we need the students' attention for them to learn and that the fewer disruptions, the more productive the learning environment.

Some of the tips presented in this book will be familiar, while others may be new. You will find yourself saying:

I do that some of the time.

or

I used to do that.

or

I should try that.

There is no magic wand, no single tip or strategy that will transform an uncooperative student or class into a model. <u>All the tips and strategies work together.</u>

The Environment

There is always an environment—both the physical and the emotional.

Physical Environment:

- Seating arrangement with walkways
- Teacher's proximity
- Teacher's desk off to the side or in the back
- Posted Behavior Plan: Expectations, Consequences, and Rewards
- Academically-rich bulletin boards
- Motivational posters
- Brag boards of students' work
- Organized materials and supplies (labeled boxes, doors, and drawers)
- Neat and clean room
- Etc.

Regardless of the students' ages or levels, walking into a well-organized classroom with some academic stimuli and a welcoming atmosphere provides a secure feeling—as if they are in good hands.

Emotional Environment:

- Safe
- Supportive
- Encouraging

The emotional environment, or tone, of the classroom is the most important component of the environment. <u>Learning is vastly impaired if students are afraid, reluctant to ask questions, or don't feel that their teacher has faith in them.</u> The next topic, "Positive Relationships," plays a major role in creating a healthy emotional environment.

TIP 1 Check your environment for both the physical and the emotional.

Positive Relationships

"Earn the Right"

B ack in 1972, in Dixon, IL, an elderly nun, who had been a teacher and an administrator for her entire career, was a keynote speaker at a district in-service day. She walked up to the podium, stood beside it, pulled the microphone down since she was less than five feet tall, and said to the audience, "If there isn't anything else that you learn from me today, you'll learn that you have to earn the right to discipline."

Of all the strategies in this book, "Earn the Right" is the most powerful. For some teachers, it is also the most difficult because it requires them to genuinely care and be able to reveal that caring to their students. This capacity and ability comes much easier for some than others.

There was a frustrated, secondary teacher who blurted out, "I'm not a touchy-feely person like Teresa," (another teacher in his school). The comment returned to him was, "You don't have to be a touchy-feely person; just see your students as individuals, not as a group or class, such as third period."

5

How is it that some of our more challenging students work and get along well with one teacher and not another? There may be many different factors here, but it's most likely because the teacher has either earned or not earned the right to discipline. The students either believe or don't believe that their teacher cares about them. (Take note here that students don't need another friend. What they do need is a caring, responsible adult.)

The major reason urban students drop out of school is because they feel that no one cares (Stipek, 2006, p. 47). Many educational experts, such as Ron Clark (2004, pp. 122-3), Robert Marzano, Ruby Payne, (2005, pp. 9, 109, & 11) and Mark and Christine Boynton, (2005, pp. 4 & 92) identify positive teacher–student relationships as a major component of effective discipline.

Without a foundation of a good relationship, students commonly resist rules and procedures along with the consequent disciplinary actions (Marzano, Marzano & Pickering 2003, p. 41).

How do teachers develop positive relationships with their students? They make daily deposits. Here are just a few ways:

1. Greet your students at the door.
2. Be a good listener.
3. Smile.
4. Have non-academic talk during non-academic time.
5. Use humor when appropriate.
6. Keep high expectations for all students.
7. Give individual help.

8. Do whatever it takes to make each student successful.

9. Call on all students equitably and coach those who falter.

10. Brag about your students.

11. Send home positive notes.

12. Be a model of respect, even when disciplining.

13. Be dependable; keep your promises.

14. Treat students fairly, not necessarily equally.

15. Attend extra-curricular events.

Do some brainstorming, and you'll probably come up with a lengthy list.

Fred Jones states, "Cooperation is voluntary. It is a gift" (Jones 2007, p. 253). Think about it. Do students really have to behave? Some actually become immune to punishment or even perceive it as getting special attention. When students are convinced that you care, they will try harder to please you. Get to know all of your students, especially the challenging ones.

Jacque, do you have any interests outside of school?

TIP 2

Earn the right to discipline.
Develop positive relationships
with your students.

"Humor"

An eighth grade student was trying to make his girlfriend laugh during class. He broke a pencil and placed half in each ear. She laughed, and the teacher told the young man to stay after class. The consequence earned was to copy, by hand, two pages of a reference book which had small print and no illustrations. It took three, 45 minute, after-school sessions to complete.

Approximately 30 years later, the same young man was now a seventh grade social studies teacher. During a lesson, he turned to see Fred in the back, left-hand corner of the seating chart with half of a pencil in his ear and the other half coming out of his nose. Fred quickly removed the pencil and got a serious look on his face.

The first thought of the teacher was to say, "I'll see you after class;" however, he told Fred to put the pencil back and had the class turn around and look. Everyone laughed. The teacher told him that his consequence was that he had to pay attention for the rest of the class period.

Fred was a challenging student. This humorous exchange strengthened his relationship with the teacher. Sometimes you just have to laugh. This was one of those times. Showing your students that you have a sense of humor humanizes you, and if not overdone, it definitely improves public relations. (In this case, it also provided a change of state. It served as a brain break.)

When do you use humor in place of a redirection or consequence? This is a personal decision. It is different for individuals, but here are some general guidelines:

1. The student isn't really hurting anyone or anything.

2. It appears to be innocent.

3. It won't destroy your lesson.

4. You have a gut feeling that it may help build a positive relationship with both the perpetrator and the other students.

5. Last, but not least, it really is funny.

Students truly appreciate teachers who can laugh at themselves and have a sense of humor.

Ouch!!! Wait a minute. Now that's funny.

TIP 3

<u>Selectively</u>, use humor in the place of redirections and consequences.

"Dignity"

A senior in high school wrote a letter to a former seventh grade teacher—five years after the fact. Here is a quote from it:

Thank you for being such a nice teacher to everyone, and being nice to me even when I got into trouble.

Ali

Frequently, when students are disciplined, they are berated or put down. The teacher zeroes in on making the student feel guilty for the misbehavior. This can be counterproductive. It impairs future cooperation. When students don't like their teachers, they are more inclined to misbehave.

A student feeling a little remorse is not a bad outcome, but more needs to be done. The correct behavior should be reviewed, an expectation should be stated, and the appropriate consequence should be defined (also enforced). Then end with a positive comment. Here is a non-example versus a correct example:

Teacher: *Max, you will not be throwing spit wads in my* (in class) *room! I won't tolerate that kind of behavior! I'll see you during lunch detention for the rest of this week!*

Vs.

Teacher: (in private)	*Max, I expect better behavior from you. You are a better kid than this. What does expectation number one state?*
Max:	*It says to be kind to others.*
Teacher:	*What does number three state, Max?*
Max:	*It says to keep hands, feet, and objects to self.*
Teacher:	*When you threw that spit wad, you violated both of those expectations. You've earned two lunch detentions beginning today. Can you do the right thing—not throw anymore spit wads?*
Max:	*Yes*
Teacher:	*Thank you, Max. I know you can do better.*

The student still earns the consequence, but his dignity is preserved. For most kids this deposit will contribute to the building of a positive, teacher–student relationship which will pay off later.

In years to come, your students may forget what you taught them, but they will always remember how you made them feel.

Author Unknown

TIP 4

Preserve your students' dignity during discipline. It's a solid deposit.

"Private Discipline"

A ninth grade algebra teacher is presenting a lesson to his class. As he looks to the back row, he sees Alfred with his book closed and iPod playing through his earphones. Mr. Stevens stops his lesson and yells, "Alfred! Put that away right now and open your book to page 79!"

Alfred hesitates. Mr. Stevens yells, "Do it now!"

Alfred fires back, "#@* you!" Mr. Stevens sends him to the office and writes a referral to be taken down by another student.

Was Alfred wrong? Yes. Was the teacher wrong? Yes.

Calling students out in front of their peers is a recipe for trouble. As professionals, we should know that. Also, note that the older students become, the more prone they are to "saving face" among their peers.

Mr. Stevens could have handled this situation in a variety of ways that may have prevented the blow up. What else might he have done?

He could have worked his way toward Alfred while looking at other students' work as he went. By the time he got to Alfred, he may have found the earphones put away and the book opened.

If not, he could have kept teaching as he stood near Alfred, pointed to his book, and made a motion to remove the earphones. Then he could have said a quiet, "Thank you," and discussed the iPod with Alfred after the lesson.

If Alfred refused to comply, Mr. Stevens could have finished the lesson and asked Alfred to step out for a quick, 1:1 conference in which Alfred would earn a consequence.

As long as a student isn't keeping you from teaching or the other students from learning, it is frequently better to let it go until you have the time to properly address it. This is particularly true for defiant students.

> *Remember, when you discipline a student, you are on a stage with the entire class as your audience. This is a critical time that reveals your true character. Your strength is in your resolve—not your mean look or your raised voice.*
>
> *J. Shaulis*

By keeping your discipline private, you will have fewer classroom disasters <u>and</u> will be respected more by your students for preserving their dignity.

TIP

5   Discipline: It's a private matter.

"Group Punishment"

There are times when light forms of group punishment are useful. How often and to what extent are the factors that separate usefulness from tearing down positive teacher–student relationships. Here is a good example of group punishment:

Teacher dismissing class from team tables:

- *Team One may line up. Team Two, I'll come back to you when your desks are straight and the scraps on the floor are picked up.* The students on Team Two monitor themselves and get the student(s) who are out of compliance to straighten their desks and pick up the scraps beneath them.

- Teacher dismisses the other teams and then comes back to Team Two to see if they are ready now. If all is neat and tidy they will be dismissed. If not, he will now focus on the individual(s) who have not complied. The group will no longer be responsible for the non-compliant. *Everyone looks good - congratulations!* or *Everyone may line up except for Joe. Joe, pick up the paper under your desk please.*

- Joe may do so or he may say, *I didn't put it there. It's not mine. I'm not going to pick it up.*

- Teacher may say, *Bring it to me, and let's see whose paper it is. Thank you, Joe. Isn't this your drawing?*

Notice that the teacher did not continue to punish the students who were following directions. He zeroed in on Joe instead, and if necessary, would use his behavior plan's consequences.

(Side note: Unless you are positive whose it is, never have students pick up facial tissues, gum, etc. Get a paper towel or piece of copy paper and dispose of it yourself.)

Teachers frequently use light forms of group punishment when they want the compliant students to help them with discipline. Two more appropriate examples:

- *We'll begin when everyone is focused.*

- *We'll continue to our special when everyone is facing forward, quiet, and has hands to their sides.*

It can be a useful tool.

Here is an example that deteriorates positive relationships—a non-example:

The teacher just collected math homework and is disappointed as to how many students either did poorly or did not complete their homework.

> *Students, I'm really disappointed with your homework. Because of your poor performance I am going to add some additional problems to tomorrow's assignment.*

Are there now some students being punished for something they did not do? Yes. When students are dealt with injustice, they become resentful, and the teacher's public relations takes a hit—especially with those who are on the fence post regarding their feelings about their teacher.

Students have lost recesses, or other privileges, made to write sentences, given extra work, etc., because of one or a few students' lack of work or misbehavior. <u>It is better to miss a student who has not complied than to punish those who were doing the right thing</u>. Using your alertness, you will eventually catch the one(s) who do not comply.

Because Miss Crabtree frequently used group punishment, her students were hoping that the new kid would be well behaved.

TIP 6 Be careful when you use your students to help you discipline - use group punishment <u>sparingly</u>.

Procedures to Routines

The number one problem in the classroom is not discipline: it's the lack of procedures and routines (Wong & Wong 2009, p. 165).

There should be a procedure for anything you have your students do on a regular basis. Having procedures in place will: (1) make the students feel more secure by knowing what to do and how to do it, (2) save time, and (3) reduce misbehaviors.

Ruby Payne states: 95% of all referrals are written during the first and last five minutes of class (Payne 2005, DVD Module 6). Unstructured time is dangerous. One of the worst violations of this is when teachers allow their students to socialize the last ten minutes of class. This is an opportunity to check the students' comprehension or reinforce the day's lesson through discussion, playing an academic game, etc.

Here are just some items that require procedures:

Entering class	Materials and supplies
Book bags	Getting a drink
Heading for assignments	Asking for classmate's help
Bell work	Sharpening a pencil

Absent work	Class and station rotations
Late work	Lining up
Handing work in	Walking in the hall
Getting the students' attention	When work is done
Getting the teacher's attention	Wrap-up
Restroom permission	Dismissal

Generally, posters are not made for procedures. There would be too many; however, if students are struggling with one, a poster may be necessary. Here are two examples:

How to Enter Class

1. Walk to assigned seat.

2. Quietly take out text, agenda, homework, and supplies.

3. Put book bag under desk.

4. Quietly complete your bell work.

When My Work Is Done

1. Complete make-up work.

2. Study vocabulary words.

3. Drill flashcards with approved classmate.

4. Read chapter book.

5. Do a bonus activity.

Your goal is to practice your procedures until they become routines. How is this accomplished? Make the procedures a priority the first month of school. Teach the procedures like a lesson: explain, model, and practice. Then, whenever one is not followed, stop, reteach if necessary, and do over. Two examples:

Class, please take your papers back. Remember to check your headings to see if everything is included like the sample on the board. Then, you pass your papers in by placing yours on top so that they can be passed back to you quickly. Let's try it again. Thank you.

<u>and</u>

Everyone go back to your seats. How do we line up? That's right - one team at a time on my signal. Let's see if we can do that so no one gets bumped.

If procedures are given priority the first month of school, they will become routines, and there will be more time for learning the rest of the year.

TIP

7

Take the time to turn your procedures into routines.

"The Quiet Signal"

In this day of academic accountability, efficient use of time is essential. As much as two to four weeks per year of instructional time is wasted in many classrooms by just trying to get students settled down and focused.

Quiet signals come in all forms: chimes, clapping rhythms, and many others. If there was a school-wide quiet signal, every teacher and aide would be reinforcing the same procedure. It could even be used in assemblies, the cafeteria, and during emergency drills.

A simple raised hand by the teacher is very effective. Just instruct the students to stop, look, and listen whenever you raise your hand. Try it out by having the students turn to a neighbor and talk. Then, you raise your hand. As they see it, they should stop, look, and listen. Practice it a couple of times. The quiet signal should work in less than five seconds. Time your students and acknowledge their successes.

If students are working with their heads down, give a single verbal cue along with it, such as *Class* or *Attention*. Only say it once. Then stand quietly with your hand held high.

Encourage students to raise their hands for their peers to see. The raised hands should ripple through the room like a wave. Sometimes older students are reluctant to copy you. It's acceptable as long as they stop, look, and listen.

A quiet signal is a non-negotiable. Students who do not comply must be held accountable. Simply write down the names of the offenders and use your behavior plan. After a couple of weeks, this procedure should become a routine.

If your current quiet signal is working and you don't want to give it up, it's okay, but also teach the raised hand and use it often enough that your students recognize it and comply. This signal can be used when you are out of the classroom, and if other staff are using the same one, it will support them.

Mr. Masoncup was known county-wide for his quiet signal.

TIP 8

Get the most out of your instructional time. Use a quiet signal.

"Only Instruct Quiet Students"

NEVER instruct while the students are talking. This is another non-negotiable.

Use your quiet signal and wait for them to focus. If you begin instruction while students are talking, you are teaching them that they don't have to be quiet when you teach. As soon as any talking begins during your instruction, stop, slowly turn to the offender(s), keep a neutral expression, and wait. If they continue, give a redirection such as, "Focus here please. Thank you," and wait. As before, if students continue, use your behavior plan. (Subtle redirections and behavior plans will be explained later.) This is a procedure for the teacher. When used consistently, it will become a routine for you.

Observe a quality, veteran teacher, and you will immediately experience that when they talk, their students listen. There will be no interruptions, and in the rare event that there is one, it will be short lived.

TIP
9
Only instruct quiet students.
Make it a routine.

"Hand Signals"

Simple hand signals by the students can save time and decrease disruptions.

If a student has to use the restroom, wants a drink, needs to sharpen a pencil, or get assistance from another student, there is no reason to slow down the lesson.

An opened, raised hand will always signify: *I have a question.* Here are four others:

- Index finger stands for: *May I use the restroom?*

- Two fingers like the traditional peace sign means: *May I get a drink?*

- A hand holding a pencil signifies: *May I sharpen my pencil?*

- Three fingers translate to: *May I ask another student a question about the current assignment?* (Ask three before me.)

An experienced teacher should be able to seamlessly acknowledge and reply to these requests during instruction.

Examples:

- You are helping a student, and you see another student raising his hand with the index finger pointing up. You simply point toward the restroom key and the student goes.

- You are in the middle of a presentation. A student holds up two fingers. You say, "Wait 'til lunch," and continue your lesson.

- You are doing small-group instruction. A student doing independent work holds up three fingers for help from another student. You give a nod of approval and continue your instruction.

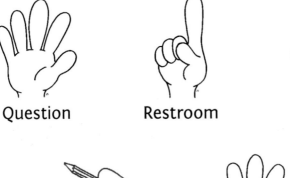

| Question | Restroom | Drink |

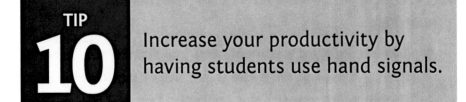

Sharpener   Ask another

TIP 10

Increase your productivity by having students use hand signals.

Presence

Here are some questions you may want to ask yourself regarding your students' behavior and your presence:

- Do they pause to say, "Hello," when entering your room?
- When you walk to the front of the room, do they begin to "settle in"—become a bit more quiet and look in your direction?
- Is your quiet signal effective?
- Are you rarely interrupted?
- Do they acknowledge your expertise?
- Are your directions followed the first time?

These questions could go on, but the bottom line is: <u>do your students recognize your leadership</u>? Do they want to follow you?

You can improve your presence through your appearance, voice, proximity, body language, and expertise.

Appearance - Distinguish yourself from your students. Be well groomed and dress professionally.

Voice - Avoid being a monotone. Use variety regarding volume and pitch. Be expressive. Never talk above the students.

Use your quiet signal and wait for their attention. Talking loudly can actually contribute to students being louder.

Proximity - Remember when you were in school? When were you most likely to talk or make a face at a peer? Maybe even throw a spit wad? Answer: When the teacher wasn't nearby. The longer you stay in one spot the more likely there will be problems from those who are far away.

Circulate as much as possible. Give every child a front-row seat by teaching among your students rather from just front and center.

The most basic factor that governs the likelihood of students goofing off in the classroom is their physical distance from the teacher's body. (Jones, 2007, p. 29)

Body Language - Your expressions and movements are powerful communicators—frequently stronger than words. Example: A student is talking during your instruction.

You say, "Amy, stop talking and pay attention."

vs.

With a neutral expression, you stop instructing, slowly turn to face Amy, and wait.

Which of the above would make the deepest impression upon you if you were the talker? Keep in mind that verbally correcting students in front of their peers often triggers unwanted responses. As the saying goes, "Sometimes less is more." (The Subtle Redirections chapter will provide additional suggestions.)

Body language can also refer to the teacher's posture. When you walk with purpose and stand tall, you are more noticeable than if you lack good posture and shuffle your feet. Shoulders back with head held high conveys confidence.

Expertise - Do you know your content? Are you well prepared? Students admire knowledge. You earn respect and presence when you are perceived as an "expert." Even younger students can detect a teacher who is not prepared.

Mr. Froelich thought of a way to improve his presence.

TIP 11

Improve your presence through: professional appearance, expressive voice, frequent proximity, use of body language, and expertise of content.

Withitness

"Withitness" is a term created by Jacob Kounin to describe the teacher's awareness of what is going on in all parts of the classroom at all times. Have you ever had a teacher who had "eyes in the back of his head?"

Sometimes more than proximity is necessary. Remember the old westerns when the gunfighter was in the saloon and would only sit with his back to the wall? That way, of course, no one could sneak up behind him, and he could keep his eyes on everyone. That same principle can be applied to managing a classroom.

Think about that student who's watching you while he is supposed to be working. What is he doing? Answer: Usually waiting for you to turn away so he can play. How can you minimize this scenario? <u>Never turn your back to your audience—face them as much as possible</u>. Be like the gunfighter.

When helping one student, carefully select a position that would enable you to see the most challenging pupils. During independent work, if there are too many trouble spots, stand behind the students and have one student come to you at a time so you can have the entire class within your range of vision.

Another routine teachers should develop is to scan the room every few minutes. This is especially true when writing on a whiteboard or ActivBoard with your back to the class. Special classrooms like the media center, computer lab, shop, etc., may even benefit from installing convex mirrors in the corners to improve supervision.

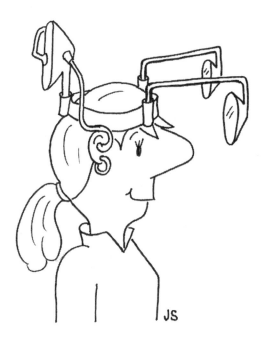

Mrs. Lewis was the first to purchase the new
Hear-All See-All from the ACME Catalog.

TIP

12 Sharpen your withitness by facing your audience.

Seating Assignments

Inform students on day one that they will always have assigned seats and that you will make any changes necessary to give them the best possible learning environment. This is an application of your withitness—to know who needs to sit where determined by their academics and behavior. <u>Never relinquish this right—it is a non-negotiable</u>.

On the first day of school, you can create seating charts using one of these three methods:

- Alphabetical order

- Random

- Heterogeneously by test data or placement card information

Let the students know that the first seating arrangement is temporary and that changes will be made throughout the year.

Since teaching became a profession, teachers have been separating their challenging students so they don't influence one another. They also surround them with good role models hoping for a positive effect.

A "five point rule" is helpful. Place the four most disruptive students in the four corners of the seating chart—not the four corners of the room. Seat the two who need the most academic assistance in the front corners and the two more academically advanced in the back corners. Corner seats have fewer neighbors, therefore, fewer distractions. It also only takes three role models to surround a student in a corner seat. Even if you arrange your students in teams, there are still four corners.

What about the fifth most attention-seeking student? It's a five point rule. That student should be assigned to the center, or near center, of the room and surrounded with compliant students. Here are two examples:

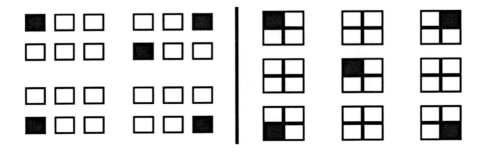

Mr. Abel, a former airline employee, had a unique way of assigning seats.

Holly, let's try you in business class.

TIP 13

Use your withitness to create the best possible learning environment.

Subtle Redirections

A few subtle cues can keep misbehaviors from snowballing. Just as teachers can respond to students' hand signals while keeping the flow of the lesson, successful teachers can also give redirections without interrupting instruction.

Here are four common redirections:

- Pause, turn, and with a neutral expression, look at the disruptor. Wait. Then resume your lesson.

- Use proximity. Without stopping your instruction walk toward the off-task student.

- Turn toward the student and simply say something like, "Do you agree, Richard?"

- Throw a whisper. Just quietly say the student's name and keep teaching.

There are also some hand signals for the teacher to use, such as:

- Finger to the mouth for quiet,

- Twirling a finger that points downward for turn around,

- Pointing toward the desk for get to work, and

- Showing a palm down for settle down.

When teachers use hand signals, they frequently have to get the students' attention first. Once again, if the student isn't looking, just throw a whisper.

<u>After any redirection always thank the students before they even comply.</u> A nod of the head, a "thumbs up," or a quiet, "Thank you," all work. Also, always visually check back a couple of times for compliance.

There are many ways to redirect students. As long as you are subtle and reinforce with a positive action or word, they should work for most of the minor misconducts. The objective is to stop the off-task behavior with a minimal amount of effort or disruption and to avoid calling students out in front of their peers or giving them "center stage."

How many redirections do you give before students earn consequences? There is no set number. It's individualized. Here is what has to be considered:

- Is the student trying to comply?
- Is the student capable of staying on task for long periods of time?
- How long did the student comply before going off task again?

TIP 14

Subtle redirections make for seamless instruction.

"The Follow-up"

Teachers who tend to lack withitness fall into a **Danger Zone** of not following up on their redirections. This is one of the worst things teachers can do. It can absolutely destroy their classroom management.

When you subtly redirect a student to turn around and pay attention, do not assume that he is going to comply simply because you attended to it. You must check back at least a couple of times to verify that the student did in fact do as directed.

When you follow-up, you are accomplishing two things: (1) the obvious, that you are making sure that the redirection you just gave is being followed, and (2) the more important one, that you are sending a message to all of your students that you have high expectations regarding their behavior and that you will follow through.

Student body language can help you follow-up. Here are three examples:

- Feet pointing toward a peer - The student intends to resume talking. Make sure that the feet are pointing forward.

- Student doing independent work is watching you - The student is looking for an opening to misbehave again.

- Hands in the desk - Is the student texting or making a spitwad?

TIP 15 Stay out of the "Danger Zone." Always follow-up on your redirections.

"Be Covert"

If a student is off task, randomly walk to other students' desks as you approach the problem. Let him think that he is just one of many being checked. Fred Jones (2007) calls this camouflage (p. 220).

When you do get to the off-task student, avoid eye contact. Focus on his work or book. If you do talk, continue to look at what he is supposed to be doing, not him.

Example:

Brian is looking at a motorcycle magazine instead of beginning his assignment. You notice this as you scan the room. You know that Brian frequently challenges his teachers anytime he is redirected, so you casually work your way back to him by looking at other students' work. When you arrive, he has put his magazine under his text.

You might say, "Let me help you get started on your assignment." (You are looking at the text and the blank paper—not him.)

He says, "I don't need any help."

You say, "The first answer is on the second page of the chapter. Just raise your hand if you get stuck."

Then you hang around helping others nearby until you are convinced that Brian is on task.

After class you might catch him before he leaves with, "Do you like motorcycles?" (Non-academic talk is a great way to build positive, teacher–student relationships.)

Note: Some students love being the center of attention and are quick to publicly say to their teacher, "What do you want?" Don't get pulled into a conversation or argument. Use the "broken record" strategy (Tip 35) with these attention-seeking pupils.

Mr. Steinman still needed more practice at being covert.

TIP 16 Avoid center stage—be covert.

"Ignoring"

There are times when younger or immature students commit small, irritating, off-task behaviors to get their teachers' attention—like tapping a pencil. There are also times when students simply do unconscious acts, such as softly humming to themselves. Teachers will usually give these types of behaviors some time before intervening.

Why would a teacher do that? The reasons would be (1) to modify pupils' behaviors, such as not responding to a student who calls out until he properly raises his hand, or (2) to not disrupt the flow of instruction.

Ignoring a misbehavior is when you are aware of it and purposely choose to wait and see if it will desist on its own—without intervention. This can be an effective strategy. Generally, it is used when the following apply:

1. You believe that it will stop without giving it attention.
2. It is not keeping you from teaching or the students from learning.
3. One or more students will benefit from it.

Of course, if it continues or disrupts instruction, it is time to implement redirections and, if necessary, begin consequences.

Use "Ignoring" to modify behaviors and to maintain instructional flow.

The Behavior Plan

A Behavior Plan is a set of posted Expectations, Consequences, and Rewards. It provides students with a code of conduct, the outcomes if they are not followed, and the benefits or privileges when they are.

Posting the Behavior Plan in a prominent place helps students to remember and understand the "rules of the game" up front. This helps avoid confusion and conflict. They know what will happen next. It also provides teachers with a consistent, sequential path to take when redirections are not enough.

Have you ever seen a teacher repeatedly redirect a student until his patience ran out? What eventually happened? He probably skipped to sending the student out to a colleague for a timeout or wrote a referral and sent him to the office.

Posted plans make it easy for teachers to reference when needed—whether to praise, correct, or reward students.

Expectations	Consequences	Rewards

Note: When teachers work on a team, having a common behavior plan benefits their students. The consistency promotes clarity.

TIP 18 Provide structure for your students and yourself. Post your behavior plan.

"Expectations"

The term "Expectations" is more positive than "Rules." When creating your classroom expectations, consider these questions:

- What behaviors do you want to see displayed?
- What makes a productive learning environment?

Each expectation should be stated clearly, briefly, and in positive language. Expectations vary among grade levels. The younger students need more specific ones than the secondary students. Here are three samples:

(Elementary)

Expectations

1. Be kind with words and actions.
2. Work and play safely.
3. Get permission to leave your seat.
4. Use indoor voices.
5. Always do your best.
6. Help keep our classroom neat and clean.

(Middle)

Expectations

1. Be kind to others.

2. Stay on task.

3. Keep hands, feet, and objects to self.

4. Respect all property.

5. Follow directions the first time.

(High)

Expectations

1. Be polite.

2. Be prompt.

3. Be prepared.

4. Be productive.

"Buy-in" is important. If you have a self-contained class-room—the same students all day—let them help create your Expectations. Then you can make posters, do some role playing, and have discussions. For the upper grades where students rotate, you can have the students brainstorm examples and non-examples of the posted Expectations along with defining and discussing them. The students need to understand what you want from them and why.

Your expectations drive everything you do in your classroom. They must be taught the first week and frequently reviewed and referenced throughout the year:

- End of the day or class: *How did we do with our expectations today?*

- During class: *This team did an exceptional job of sharing and supporting one another. That is Expectation #1.* (Point to it.) *Way to go!*

TIP 19 Teach your expectations, and refer to them daily.

"Good Character"

Grades will always be important. Parents, children, and universities value them. Awards and scholarships are earned from them. What could be more important in school? The answer is character.

What is character? Here are just a few words you will find in its definition: honesty, integrity, courage, and moral strength. Some people say it is what you do when no one is looking.

Teachers' role:

- Praise and/or reward students for displaying good character. Example: *Jessica, I saw the way you helped Mrs. Wallick. That was very nice of you.*

- Use the phrase, *"What should you have done?"* in 1:1 conferences.

- Frequently reference examples of good character. Example: *Why do you think the main character chose to stay and risk being hurt?*

- Be a model for your students.

There was a teacher who would begin each school year with this question for the class: *"What is your most valuable possession?"* After the students were given some think time, answers like these were given: "My skate board," "My computer," "My dog," etc. Then the teacher would say, "What about your character?" Next, the teacher would pose these questions for discussion:

- *What is character?*
- *Why is it important?*
- *Who gives you character?*
- *Who can take it away?*

Hopefully, the students would get the idea that they alone control their character.

The same teacher would use the phrase, *"Was that showing good character?"* whenever students made poor choices.

One of his students was teasing a classmate. He observed it and walked over to her. Before anything was said by the teacher, the young lady said, "I know. I know. That wasn't showing good character." She immediately went over to the student she was teasing and said, "I'm sorry. I should not have said that." The teacher simply smiled and gave the student a nod of approval.

Whether the students are those who generally behave well or those who frequently challenge teachers, both populations can benefit from the "sale" of good character.

You can lose everything you own, but if you have good character, you can recover. Hard work and honesty will always be valued.

TIP 20 Hold high expectations for your students by promoting "Good Character."

"Consequences"

After you feel that a student has had an appropriate number of redirections, inform him that he has earned his "official warning." <u>Students never earn more than one warning</u>. A frequent error teachers make is giving more than one and/or going back to redirections after the "official warning" has been issued.

Make sure that students know what comes next if they choose to continue. This can be accomplished by asking a student, "Do you know what comes next?" or stating, "Do the right thing. I don't want to see you go to number two," (meaning the second consequence). Both the teacher and the student are now locked into the numbered consequences. The only exception is if a severe misbehavior occurs which would necessitate skipping steps.

Assigning a consequence is never pleasant, but if all you do is redirect or give warnings, the result is an out-of-control classroom.

How do you create your consequences?

1. <u>Brainstorm</u> all possible consequences.

2. <u>Screen</u> your list to check if they are (a) appropriate for the age group, (b) acceptable by administration, (c) <u>comfortable enough for you to use</u>, (d) manageable, and (e) economical regarding your time and effort.

3. <u>Prioritize</u> the remaining ones from least to most severe.

4. <u>Determine the number needed</u>, and <u>select</u> the ones you want.

Here are two examples. Notice the statements above and below the consequences. These are generally included for grades 3-12.

Consequences

Redirections __may__ be given. If not followed, consequences will be earned.

1. Warning.
2. 5 min. off recess/activity
3. 10 min. off recess/activity
4. Timeout seat
5. Parent note
6. Timeout class and parent call
7. Referral to principal or counselor

Severe misbehaviors go directly to higher consequences.

Consequences

Redirections __may__ be given. If not followed, consequences will be earned.

1. Warning.
2. Brief 1:1 conference
3. "Seat of Opportunity"
4. Detention
5. Alternative room & parent contact
6. Referral to administrator or counselor

Severe misbehaviors go directly to higher consequences.

CONSEQUENCES

1. Official warning
2. Second official warning
3. I'm-not-kidding official warning
4. I-really-mean-it official warning
5. Probation
6. Double probation
7. I'm telling!!!

JS

Mr. Waverly hoped that he would never have to use the seventh consequence.

TIP 21

Create, post, and use consequences for those who do not accept redirections.

"One-to-one Conferences"

An early step on a behavior plan's consequences can be a brief, teacher–student conference—a one-to-one.

For example: the student may have already been given a couple of redirections. Then the teacher says, "Nancy, that's your warning." Nancy continues to make fun of her classmates. The teacher issues the second consequence, the 1:1. Nancy now knows that she will have a face-to-face talk with her teacher as soon as the lesson is over or after class.

The 1:1 can be an effective consequence if the teacher follows these steps:

1. Keep it as private as possible.

2. Pretend that the parents are standing behind the student. (This creates a more professional mindset.)

3. Have the student face you. Encourage but do not demand eye contact.

4. Remove or position the student so she cannot see her classmates. (An audience can evoke a negative or flippant attitude.)

5. Keep a neutral expression.

6. Ask the student, "How can I help you?" Pause. Then say, "I don't want to see you earn anymore consequences."

7. Wait. Let the student go into a "discomfort zone."

8. Use positive talk. Let the student know what is expected of her: "Nancy, you know how to be polite. I expect you to treat your classmates with respect." (Use Tip 32: "Questions")

9. Ask the student what the next consequence is. If she does not respond, then inform her.

10. Give encouragement, such as, "Nancy, I know you can be a kind person."

11. If the student continues her misbehavior, go onto the next consequence(s).

Sometimes the misbehavior recurs before the 1:1 can take place. Just go onto the next consequence. You can still have the 1:1 later.

This mini-conference should not take more than two minutes.

When students display an I-don't-care attitude, simply make them aware of the upcoming consequences, and move on. You could close by saying, "You are a better young lady/man than this. I hope you make the right decision."

TIP 22 When used correctly, the 1:1 conference is an effective, early consequence.

"Timeouts"

R elocating a student is a common consequence. Here are two examples of Timeout:

- Teacher sends a student to an isolated place <u>in the room</u> to cool down and rethink behavior.

- Teacher sends a student to an isolated place <u>out of the room</u> to cool down and rethink behavior (to a colleague— <u>not</u> out in the hall without supervision). This is usually used as a last resort before the student earns a referral. The teacher is obligated to contact parents whenever the child is removed from the regular educational setting.

There are three expectations for timeout:

Timeout

1. Stay seated.
2. Be quiet.
3. Raise hand for help.

Placing a sign near the Timeout Seat is a good idea.

A variation of a timeout is the <u>Seat of Opportunity</u>. This is more commonly used in grades 4–12. It is generally used as an early consequence. The teacher sends a student to a desk off to the side as a physical reminder that he needs to settle down. The student still faces the teacher and continues to participate. This needs to be explained to the students beforehand. Let them know that you will quietly point to another desk and say "Thank you." It is not meant to embarrass them but just to give them an opportunity to settle down and not earn the next consequence.

Timeout can also be used as a quick intervention for elementary students. Example: Suzie is calling out without raising her hand. She isn't being mean. She is simply being impulsive. The teacher can say, "Suzie, take five." Suzie goes to a different seat or just stands off to the side or back of the room. <u>This is not a consequence on the behavior plan</u>, but just a short time to rethink/refocus. The teacher can call her back at any time, but it doesn't go past five minutes. With primary students, two minutes would be sufficient. Regard this the same way you would a redirection.

If you are going to use this brief timeout as an intervention, as stated before, you must explain and model it to your students. Tell them that it is not a punishment. It is simply a way to remind students of the Classroom Expectations. Call it "Take Five" to avoid confusion.

Timeout strategies and their variations go by different names: Classroom Timeout, Out-of-Class Timeout, Alternative Room Placement, Time and Space Place, Cool Down Zone, etc. What matters is that the students know what they're called and understand the expectations that go along with each of them.

Mr. Rock didn't understand the concept of the timeOUT chair. Fortunately, Scooter is okay and was the only student to experience it. (Mr. Rock is no longer with the district.)

TIP 23

Timeouts are effective discipline strategies.

"Rewards"

There are two types of rewards: planned and spontaneous. Planned rewards are those that are agreed upon in advance. They are given conditionally. These can be given to the whole class or individuals.

Examples:

- *Every time the class has read 100 books, we will celebrate by having a pizza party for lunch.*

- *If we have time at the end of today's lesson, we can play South American Bingo.*

- *Dennis, every morning you accomplish your goal this week, you may choose a friend to have lunch with outside.*

Spontaneous rewards are the kind given when you catch a student doing the right thing. They can be used to promote good social skills, such as: sharing, helping others, and being polite. They can also nurture good work habits, such as: being on time and bringing required materials. Examples:

- *Trisha, helping Sonya pick up her crayons was very thoughtful of you. Here is a sticker for your Good Citizen Chart. One more sticker and you'll be ready to go to the treasure chest.*

- *I just gave tickets to all of those who came to class on time and immediately began their bell work. Way to go!*

The spontaneous rewards are particularly effective in shaping and reinforcing good social skills in elementary students.

Rewards are posted just like expectations and consequences:

Rewards	**Rewards**
Be proud.	Take pride in your accomplishments.
Learn more.	
Earn privileges:	Get better grades.
Stickers, center time, teacher helper, game with a friend, Super Note, and more	Earn privileges:
	Homework pass, media center or computer lab pass, project with a partner, etc.

Screen your rewards just as you would your consequences: age appropriate, administration approved, comfortable to use, manageable, and economical regarding both time and effort.

It is easy to go overboard with rewards. Don't create something that is too difficult to administer or ends up with students only working for the rewards. Hopefully, <u>the best reward a child can earn is learning something new and your praise.</u>

TIP 24

Brainstorm rewards that would motivate your students.

Note: The next three reward strategies are intended for elementary teachers. They could be adapted for self-contained, secondary students.

"Reward Strip"

This is a spontaneous reward strategy that has been used by many elementary teachers. A simple strip of paper is taped to the students' desks, folders, or agendas. Whenever a student's Reward Strip fills up with credits represented by stamps, stickers, or teacher's initials, it becomes a ticket for the treasure chest, which is filled with items, such as: school supplies, coupons from contributors, passes for privileges, such as: computer time, academic game with an <u>approved</u> friend, special place to have lunch, etc.

A child earns a credit whenever the teacher catches him doing a good deed or making an exceptional effort. (Self-inking stamps are convenient. They can be ordered at any office supply store. The cost may be as much as $25, but they are cheaper than some stickers, and they save time.)

The number of squares is your option. As behaviors improve, you could also add more squares to "raise the bar." Here are two possible reward strips with clip art added to increase motivation.

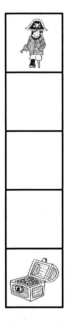
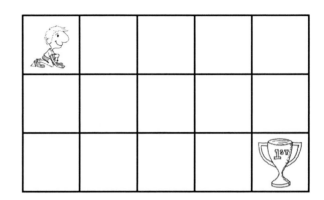

Never take back credits. Not earning credits is a consequence in itself. The posted classroom's consequences still apply—they are still earned.

If used as a planned reward rather than a spontaneous one, do so with individual students rather than the whole class. They could earn a credit for every incident-free lesson. Do <u>not</u> use this strategy every 30 minutes or after every lesson with too many students at a time. There was a second grade teacher who ran around after every lesson giving stamps to all who stayed on task. She was wearing herself out. Teachers deserve better.

TIP 25

Reward Strips can be incentives for younger students.

"Reward Ladder"

A Reward Ladder is similar to the Reward Strip, but the elementary students do the work of advancing their pins rather than the teacher walking around and giving credits. The teacher simply says something like, "Tim, you may move your pin. Thank you for helping Angela with her project."

This concept works well when you have the same class all day long. It has also been successful with a team of two teachers who share two classes. Simply have two ladders in each room.

How to make a Reward Ladder:

1. Select different colors of 9 X 12 construction paper. (Five to eight colors works best—your choice.)

2. Fold the colored sheets vertically/ hamburger to determine overlap lines.

3. Half lap them using a glue stick. The black at the top will fold over the purple like a tent making it a little thicker.

4. Run the ladder through a laminator.

5. Use a paper punch to make two holes at the top. (Now you can hang it so students can place their clips on it.)

6. Buy a pack of wooden clothespins.

7. Lay the pins out so half of them face the other half. This way you will always have half the pins on each side of the ladder with no one's name upside down.

8. Now use a permanent marker to print the names on the top sides.

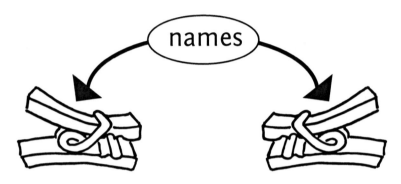

How it works:

1. Place all pins on green, start. (Pins can even clamp onto other pins if necessary.)

2. As students comply, do courteous acts, etc., the teacher can say, "You may move your pin." Some students may get to move their pin two times in a day while others may move only once or not at all. (Two moves maximum per day works well. Use just verbal praises after a child has moved his pin twice.)

3. Each color represents a reward. Here are some possible examples:

   - **Orange** = sticker (first color after start)
   - **Blue** = treat
   - **Yellow** = picture (Search images & print)
   - **Turquoise** = computer time
   - **Red** = academic game with <u>approved</u> friend

- **Purple** = neat seat (soft cushion for their chair)
- **Stars** = treasure chest (top of ladder)

4. The stickers and treats can be immediate rewards. The student walks to the sticker box and selects one. (Don't have too many choices of stickers.) For treats, tongs to reach into a jar of pretzels, graham crackers, etc. work well.

5. Pictures can be printed from computer images: animals, cars, sports, etc. Place four on a sheet, laminate, and cut for individual pictures. Students can tape one picture at a time onto their desks.

6. Other rewards, like using the computer and the academic game with a friend, have to be determined by the teacher so they don't disrupt the day's lessons. Students could be given a ticket to hold until the appropriate time (generally the first or last ten minutes of the day).

7. Some students may want to save their "neat seat" for the next day so they can enjoy it longer. It's their choice—the rest of today or all day tomorrow. (At the time of this writing, WalMart was selling chair cushions with rubber backings that prevent sliding for

★★★
Purple
Red
Turquoise
Yellow
Blue
Orange
Green

Start at green and work upward to the stars

under $9 each.) Students can also use them when they go to the carpet for instruction.

8. When a child reaches the stars, he gets to draw from the treasure chest and moves back to start (green) to begin climbing the ladder again.

9. <u>Students are never moved down the ladder.</u> Their consequence is not moving up.

Expectations are still taught, modeled, and frequently reviewed. Consequences are explained and used when necessary. The Reward Ladder complements the behavior plan as spontaneous rewards.

It takes a little preparation and maintenance, but the Reward Ladder works <u>very</u> well when used consistently and is taught as a procedure that becomes a routine. An observer will barely notice its use, and instructional flow will not be disrupted.

TIP 26 A Reward Ladder is a great way to spontaneously reward all of your students.

Thanks go to Amanda Thorsen, 3rd grade teacher at Taylor Ranch Elementary School, Venice, Florida, who uses this concept very successfully.

"Marble Jar"

A plastic jar with marbles is a common site in many elementary classrooms. Usually, it represents a whole-group reward system. It can be either spontaneous or planned.

Examples of how a class can earn a marble:

Spontaneous:

1. When another teacher or visitor compliments the class

2. When a class was perfectly behaved during an assembly or drill

3. Anytime the students' behavior is exceptional

Planned:

Stated to the students beforehand:

1. *If we complete today's lesson with no more than two interruptions, we can add a marble to our jar.*

2. *Let's see if the class can earn a marble this morning by following expectation #3 - Get permission to leave your seat.*

3. *Whenever you can line up quietly and orderly the first time, you can earn a marble for the class.*

When the marble jar fills up to a drawn line or the top (teacher's prerogative), a reward is earned, such as: a popcorn party, an academic game, teacher brings cookies for a treat, etc.

This reward system uses peer pressure to improve behavior. Teachers have to be careful not to "set up" students who struggle with their behavior. Praise when a marble is earned but don't dwell on it when one is not. If one student regularly ruins it for all, just use the behavior plan with that student and don't let him ruin it for the others.

TIP 27

A marble jar can be used as an incentive for good behavior.

"Rewards for Older Students"

When students get to the upper grades of middle and high school, they generally have different types of reward systems than elementary students, unless they are in a self-contained classroom with the same teacher all day long. This doesn't mean that they still can't earn rewards.

What do older students like?

- Smiley faces on their papers
- Cookies or donuts
- Academic games
- Homework passes (Teacher determines for which assignments they can be used.)
- Computer time (Approved sites only)
- Media passes to work on projects with classmates (pairs only)
- Fast food coupons (Some local businesses will contribute if asked.)
- Free lunches (Some schools have student-run cafes. If so, contact their sponsor and make a deal for a few lunch passes.)

- <u>Concession credits</u> (Make a deal with the sponsor of the school's events' concessions.)

- <u>School event tickets</u>

- Etc.

Possible ways to earn planned and spontaneous rewards:

- Strong efforts receive a smiley face.

- Four consecutive school days of everyone being present earns cookies or donuts for the class on the fifth day. The days can be from two different weeks. Exempt any students who have a legitimate, chronic condition. (As before, don't dwell on the misses—just celebrate the wins.)

- On days when instruction is completed early, play an academic game.

- Any student who completes all homework for one half of a grading period (usually 4 1/2 weeks) earns a homework pass.

- Whenever a student completes assigned seat work early, and does not owe any assignments, computer time on an <u>approved</u> site is earned.

- Students who are up-to-date on their school work can be excused from class and go to the media center to create a presentation relating to the current topic of study. They must agree on a topic and the number of classes needed with the teacher. (A <u>specific</u> topic with one visual aid and no more than three class periods works well.) All well-behaved students who put forth a good effort and have regular attendance are eligible. This does require cooperation of the person running the media center. (A social studies teacher frequently had two students from each of his classes doing this for each unit of study.) It is advised that if you use this, require these students to report to your class for both attendance and dismissal.

- Coupons, free lunches, concession credits, and school event tickets could be rewards for individual students with perfect attendance for the quarter, all homework on time for the semester, etc.

TIP 28 Older students enjoy rewards too.

An entire book could be written on reward systems. Teachers have creatively developed many. Just keep the following in mind:

- Spontaneous rewards promote good choices.
- Planned rewards for the whole class can be helpful, but be careful not to let one student ruin it for all. Just use your behavior plan with that student.
- Planned rewards for individuals should be carefully developed. (This topic will be covered in a later section.)
- Keep rewards "reasonable" for both yourself and the students.

The Non-compliant

When children cannot read or write, we teach them.
When children cannot behave, we punish them.
(Paraphrased from Stephen Peters, HOPE conference, 2007)

Punishment alone does not change behavior. We also need to teach acceptable behaviors to the non-compliant—those who frequently misbehave.

Change requires additional time, energy, and patience from the teacher. Relationship building, procedures and routines, presence, withitness, subtle redirections, and behavior plans are sometimes not enough with this population.

This is where you start:

1. Read the student's cumulative folder.

2. If possible, talk with <u>both</u> past and present teachers of the child.

3. Meet with the parent(s)/guardian(s).

4. Look for any resources that may be lacking.

5. Record anecdotes including day, time, and what set the student off.

6. Identify triggers and patterns.

7. Continue to work at building a positive relationship with the student. Be patient.

8. Consider an individual behavior contract using SMART goals. (Specific, Measureable, Attainable, Relevant, and Time-bound)

9. If a contract is going to be used, get a relative or other significant person to support it.

10. Carefully surround or pair up the student with "model" peers.

11. Catch the student being good. Praise and reward. (Keep your praise private for older students—generally sixth to twelfth graders, but this may vary with individuals.)

12. Stay professional—never give up.

Students are usually the way they are for a reason. If you can't eliminate the cause, look for a lever—a carrot to motivate the child.

All of the previous chapters' tips will definitely help with this population—especially those in "Positive Relationships" and "Subtle Redirections." The following tips will provide you with some additional strategies to use with the non-compliant.

TIP 29

Be patient when working with the non-compliant. (Q·tip: quit taking it personally.)

"Composure"

When elementary teachers become upset most of their students become frightened, and when secondary teachers lose their tempers many of their students think it's funny. Becoming angry in front of your students may make you feel better at the time, but it really isn't very productive. <u>When you can handle difficult situations in a calm, professional manner, you earn respect and show that you are in control.</u>

Once you allow yourself to become upset, it takes time to settle down—approximately 27 minutes (Jones, 2007, p. 174). For many people, their pitch of voice changes and often their hands tremble enough that they have to struggle to draw a straight line or write out a referral. Their delivery becomes impaired.

Here are three quotes from Fred Jones (2007) that really put keeping your composure into perspective:

- *It takes one fool to backtalk. It takes two fools to make a conversation out of it.* (p. 224)

- *Emotions are contagious. You will get exactly what you give.* (p. 181)

- *Calm is strength. Upset is weakness.* (p. 180)

Arguments don't generally last when only one party is doing all the work, yet teachers frequently relinquish control by arguing with students. You are the adult—the professional. Here are some tips for keeping your composure with a non-compliant student: They will help you "tune out" and not get drawn into an argument.

1. <u>Imagine that the parents are in the room.</u>

2. <u>Breathe slowly</u> and relatively shallow as if you were watching TV or reading (Jones, 2007, pp.180-1).

3. <u>Relax your jaw muscles</u> (Jones, 2007, p. 203).

4. <u>Stay silent</u> (Jones, 2007, p. 225). The student will usually begin repeating or run out of steam.

5. Once you understand what the student wants, <u>focus on a point between the eyebrows</u> (Jones, 2007, Session 9).

6. <u>Tune them out</u> (Jones, 2007, Session 9) by thinking of a pleasant place or making a list: grocery items, names of candy bars, brands of cars, etc.

7. <u>Keep a calm expressionless face</u> (Jones, 2007, p.181).

This really works! Each time you use it, it will become easier. After the student is "spent," make a brief statement such as: "We'll talk after class." Use Broken Record, Tip 35 if needed.

After realizing that Patti had just deleted all of her files, Mrs. Rivera had to go to her "happy place" to keep her composure.

TIP
30
Keep your composure.
Stay in control.

"Walk in Their Shoes"

We've all heard the idiom, "Walk a mile in my shoes." This of course translates to: "You should try to understand me before criticizing me."

When a student is defiant, the misbehavior usually isn't new—not even for a kindergartener. Most of the time, there is history of poverty, poor parenting, spoiling, some type of abuse, or drug/alcohol addiction.

During the times when you find yourself face-to-face with a disobedient student, thinking of the child's life, family, lack of resources, etc., can also help you maintain your composure.

There was a defiant middle school student who was earning frequent consequences on his team. One of the teachers got to know the student and found out that the boy's mother had left him, his younger sister and his father a year or so ago and that dad remarried a woman who had two little girls.

Since they lived in a small house, the young man had to give up his room for the stepsisters and was given a cot on the lanai/porch. Having a mother leave you, getting a new stepmother, bringing two new siblings into the house, and losing your room to them, just may alter your outlook on life.

<u>The young man still earned a few consequences</u>, but the teachers extended extra help and had more patience with him. The result was that the rest of the year went much better for both him and his teachers.

TIP 31 The next time you have non-compliant children, try taking a "Walk in Their Shoes."

"Questions"

Some students see themselves as adults/equals and resent being told what to do by school staff. Think of a fellow teacher presenting an in-service at your school. The teacher stops, looks at you, and says, *"Pat, put those papers away, sit up straight, and pay attention."* You would be mortified if you were corrected by a peer in front of your fellow staff members. You may even say something back or get up and walk out of the workshop.

When students find themselves...

- taking care of another family member like a sibling or grandparent,
- cooking for themselves,
- doing their own laundry,
- working a part-time job, and/or
- simply being allowed to argue with adults in their family unit,

...they may see themselves as equals. With this mindset, they probably feel like you would have felt during the teacher in-service when you were corrected.

Does this mean that you should avoid disciplining these students? No. Try this instead: do it privately and use questions rather than directives. This approach sounds more adult, is less confrontational, and builds responsibility.

Here are some examples:

- *What else could you have done?*
- *What are the choices?*
- *What should you be doing?*
- *Do you remember the expectation?*
- *What should happen now?*

If a student doesn't reply or shrugs his shoulders, give him think time. Still nothing? Then offer some suggestions.

TIP 32 Try using questions when correcting adult-defying students.

Adapted from Ruby Payne's "The Adult Voice" (Payne, 2005, p.84-5).

"Choices"

Have you ever observed a teacher telling a student what needs to be done and what will happen if it isn't? Example: *Nicole, you either complete your work now or you'll be doing it during recess.* When teachers say "do this or else" to students, it can be interpreted as a threat or challenge, which may result in conflict.

By simply changing the wording, students will get the intended message without feeling like they have been backed into a corner. Try offering two choices, even though one is a consequence. Students will feel that they have some control and are more inclined to comply. This format comes from Kagan's Win-Win Discipline. It is called "Language of Choice" (Kagan, Kyle, & Scott, 2004, p. 14.50).

There are four steps:

1. State responsible behavior. *You need to turn around and focus*

2. State consequence. *or you can move to the "seat of opportunity."*

3. Say, "It's your choice." *It's your choice.*

4. Give encouragement. *I'm sure that you'll make the right one.*

Here is an example in which the choices are repeated for clarification:

Hal, you have two choices:

You can use the computer the "right" way

<u>or</u> *you can make the graphs using pencil and paper.*

It's your choice.

Computer or pencil and paper

I know that you'll make the right choice.

Be patient. Some students refuse to comply immediately but will eventually make the right choice if given some time and space.

As with all discipline, the delivery is crucial. A neutral expression and a calm demeanor work best.

Also, be prepared to follow through with the alternative if needed.

TIP 33 Try giving non-compliant students choices followed by encouragement.

"Time and Space"

Atypical error that a teacher can make after redirecting a student or offering choices is standing over him, waiting for compliance. This is a form of challenging the student in front his peers. As stated earlier, you may want to check on students nearby as in "Be Covert" (Tip 16), but don't be like a vulture hovering over its prey.

Give some time and space. Non-compliant students frequently need both. <u>When teachers give some room and wait, these students generally comply as long as they are convinced that their teacher will follow up if they don't.</u> Some teachers will quietly return after a couple of minutes and say something like, "Matt, do the right thing." Of course, if compliance is not achieved, use the discipline plan and go to the next step.

TIP 34

Time and Space can improve the chances of students accepting redirections or consequences.

"The Broken Record"

The broken record is an old strategy that has been around for many years. It's used when a person does not wish to engage in a conversation or an argument and simply repeats a phrase or a command. Teachers generally use it when a student is persistent about something he wants even though the procedure or rule has already been explained or established.

From an observer's point of view, it can appear to be cold and uncaring like the following non-example:

Student: *Can I go to the media center?*
Teacher: *Not now.*
Student: *I really need to go.*
Teacher: *Not now.*
Student: *Why?*
Teacher: *Not now.*
Student: Shakes her head and goes back to her seat.

Here is a way it can be used without breaking down the teacher–student relationship. <u>Begin with a statement of understanding or caring</u>. If the teacher above had begun with: "The quiz is over in two minutes. I don't want you to miss today's lesson," then began the broken record, it may have eventually ended with a reluctant "Okay."

Two examples:

Student: *Can Ruth and I work together?*
Teacher: *I understand how you like to work with Ruth, but this is an individual project. You'll do a good job on your own.*
Student: *We'll do a really good job.*
Teacher: *You'll do a good job on your own.*
Student: *We'll be quiet.*
Teacher: *You'll do a good job on your own.*

Student: *I need help. I don't understand this stuff.*
Teacher: *I want to help you, Don, but you need to return to your desk and raise your hand.*
Student: *I don't get it.*
Teacher: *You need to return to your desk and raise your hand.*
Student: *What's the first step?*
Teacher: *You need to return to your desk and raise your hand.*

Once again, the way it is delivered is important. A calm, yet firm tone with a moderate volume, a neutral expression, and eye contact works best. A broken record can often divert an argument.

TIP 35 Try using the "broken record" strategy, beginning with a statement of understanding or caring.

"Postponing"

Postponing a talk with a student has advantages:

- Gives one or both parties an opportunity to settle down if needed

- Provides teachers think time to consider possible solutions or consequences that may be needed

- Offers more time to talk in a more conducive setting

Two scenarios:

1. In front of the whole class, a student makes fun of another student's speech impediment. The student being ridiculed is embarrassed, and you're very upset. Instead of losing your temper, you simply say, "Billy, I'll see you after class."

This gives you an opportunity to cool down and think of a suitable solution—one that includes an apology as part of the consequence. Also, the class knows that something is going to happen.

2. You are just beginning a lesson when a student who is crying comes up to you. She is upset over her last test score. You say, "Jolene, this is too important to discuss now. Let's talk after class when we can give it more time."

This makes the student feel better because another person cares. It permits you to teach, provides more time to talk, and once again, gives you some think time.

Notice the phrase: <u>This is too important to discuss now</u>. That wording provides validation to students. Sometimes small things are very significant to them.

Postponing teacher–student talks can avert impulsive mistakes and contribute to better decision-making. This strategy is similar to "Table the Matter" (Kagan, Kyle, & Scott, 2004, p.14.75).

TIP 36 Use the postponing strategy when tempers run high or more time is needed.

"Sharing Experiences"

Have you ever had someone tell you that he understands why you are upset? If he shared with you an account of how he had a similar experience, it probably made you feel better. Letting someone know that you understand generally helps that person to settle down.

Teachers have three ways of sharing with their students:

1. You have had a similar experience yourself.

2. You have had other students with a similar experience.

3. You observed and shared your feelings about what you saw.

Here are three examples:

- *Debbie, I understand how you feel, I was bullied when I was in school too. It made me feel very angry.*

- *Zack, I have had a few students who were in the same situation as you.*

- *Wes, I saw what Chris did to you. I would be upset too.*

Showing understanding makes students feel that they are not alone. They may still earn a consequence, but they are more likely to settle down.

TIP 37 Remember that Sharing Experiences can help a student get through a problem.

"Tally Card"

A tally card is meant to be used with one student. It can be a way to promote self-awareness of a single misbehavior, or it can become a behavior contract used to change one misbehavior at a time. Either the teacher or the student can record the tallies. Having a brief conference after each day/class, discussing the frequency of the misbehavior, and offering praise when earned may be enough to improve the behavior. For some students, however, a contract may be needed. (Generally, as the behaviors improve, so will the grades.) Here are the steps:

1. Identify the misbehavior. Example: talking out in class

2. Collect baseline data before beginning the contract.

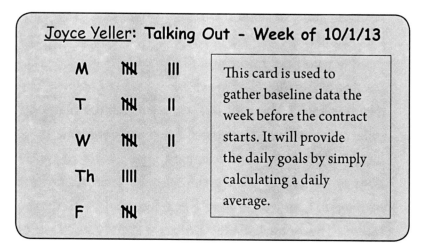

Joyce Yeller: Talking Out - Week of 10/1/13		
M	|||||	|||
T	|||||	||
W	|||||	||
Th	||||	
F	|||||	

This card is used to gather baseline data the week before the contract starts. It will provide the daily goals by simply calculating a daily average.

3. Use SMART goals:

- The behavior to improve is identified—talking out in class. It's <u>specific</u>.

- Tallies will be recorded. It's <u>measureable</u>.

- Six will be the first target (daily average = 6.2). It's <u>attainable</u>.

- It is important for the child to learn proper classroom etiquette. The child, the classmates, and the teacher will all benefit. It's <u>relevant</u>.

- Each day will be tallied, and after each week the next week's goal will be updated. It's <u>time-bound</u>.

4. Hold first teacher–student conference. It may go like this:

Joyce, I'm concerned about how frequently you yell or talk out in class during the lessons. I don't want to see you earning consequences or going on to next year's teachers with that type of behavior. I know that you can do better. I am going to place this card on your desk every class period you come this week. During the lesson, whenever I point to your desk I want you to place a tally mark next to the day of the class. Let me show you what I mean. (You demonstrate.) *You will not get consequences this week unless you really go overboard. I just want you to become aware of how often you interrupt, and I want to collect data so we can set up a good behavior contract for you next week. Can you do that?* (Teacher could also do the tallies. The behavior may improve simply because of the self-awareness.)

```
┌─────────────────────────────────────────────┐
│  Joyce Yeller: Talking Out - Week of 10/1/13  │
│                                               │
│    M                                          │
│                                               │
│    T                                          │
│                                               │
│    W                                          │
│                                               │
│    Th                                         │
│                                               │
│    F                                          │
└─────────────────────────────────────────────┘
```

5. A second teacher–student conference is held after the baseline data is collected.

- Explain how you calculated the daily goal of six for the first week. If the misbehavior has already improved, give praise. Let the student know that the goal will be revised each week and that your expectation is to reduce the daily frequency each time.

- Next, discuss rewards. Try to come up with three to four so they can be rotated each week. (Rewards become stale when overused.) You may agree on things like: lunch in a special place with a friend, computer time, media center pass with an approved classmate, or working with an approved study buddy. (Rewards have to be valued by the student, and they have to be economical and manageable for you.)

- Another index card becomes the contract which will be revised each week with the expectation of reducing the frequency.

- Review and sign the behavior contract.

> **Joyce Yeller**: Talking Out - Week of 10/8/13
>
> M   Goal = 6 or less / day
>
> T   Outside lunch with
>
> W   friend earned.
>
> Th   *Joyce Yeller*
>
> F   *Mr. Smith*

6. Is there someone with whom the student would like to share her success other than you, like a parent, another teacher (past or present), an administrator, etc.? If there is someone who would be willing to be a cheerleader/mentor to the student, use him. Simply send the child with a brief note stating that she made her goal that day or week. (Arrange what would be the best times with the "significant" person.)

7. If the parents aren't already involved, inform them of what you are doing as long as they are capable of celebrating the successes and not administering harsh discipline. If parents are going to provide additional rewards, encourage them to be modest ones. The verbal praise and support is the most important.

8. If you want a formal contract, you can use something like the following:

Behavior Contract for Joyce Yeller, 10/1/13

I will try my best not to "talk out" and interrupt instruction.

For every day that I do not call out more than _____ times, I will earn a reward. I understand that the frequency may be reduced each week.

Student_____

Parent _____

Teacher _____

The Tally Card for awareness or for a contract can be used with students from grades three to twelve. The ultimate goal is to work them off the card. There may be some weeks that the goal does not change. Maintaining the improved behaviors requires positive teacher--student relationships and continued verbal and non-verbal praise.

TIP 38 Try using a Tally Card when your behavior plan isn't enough.

"Self-Reflection"

Self-reflection does improve some students' behavior. The following form has been successfully used at the secondary level.

DAILY EFFORT GRADE

English I
Subject

Rob A.
Student

2 / 4 / 13
Week of

	Pts.	M	T	W	Th	F
Good Start:						
Bell work effort	0-2	1	2	0	1	2
Productive class work:						
1st half of class	0-3	2	3	3	3	3
2nd half of class	0-3	3	3	3	2	3
Good Finish:						
Wrap-up effort	0-2	2	2	2	2	1
Possible points =	0-10	8	10	8	8	9
Daily %:		80%	100%	80%	80%	90%

Note: Student input is very important, but the teacher makes final decision on points earned.

Daily total percentages:
- 10 = 100%
- 9 = 90%
- 8 = 80%
- 7 = 70%
- 6 = 60%
- 5 = 50%
- 4 = 40%

Week's average %

86%

Rob Anderson
Student

Mrs. Brown
Teacher

Julia Anderson
Parent/Guardian

Good Start & Finish:
2 = I stayed on task and followed all directions.
1 = I was on task some of the time.
0 = I was not on task.

Productive class work:
3 = I stayed on task and followed all directions.
2 = I stayed on task and followed directions most of the time.
1 = I was off task more than I was on task.
0 = I was not on task.

J.Shaulis 2010

98

When the teacher explains this form to the students, the following points are stressed:

- The class period is divided into four segments: bell work, first half of class, second half of class, and wrap-up.

- The teacher will briefly stop class at the conclusion of each segment. During this time, students will record what they feel they deserve. The range of possible points is in the first column.

- At the end of class, students will total their daily effort points and hand in their sheets as they leave.

- The teacher has a master sheet for tallying loss of points and reserves the right to change the students' points.

- The next school day, the sheets will be handed out for continued use. At that time, students will see if their previous day's total was approved or revised.

- At the end of each week, the students' weekly averages will be recorded as Daily Effort Grades.

Unless you have small classes, this self-reflection form is not intended to be used in all of them. It is meant for that one class that needs an additional incentive. The teacher could even give out a small, daily or weekly reward for those who achieve 90% or better.

Here is an example of the teacher's master sheet:

TEACHER'S RECORD OF STUDENTS' EFFORTS
(Tallies represent point deductions.)

Pd.	Rob	Mary	Jenny	Nick	Zoe	Jared	Noah	Keira	Evan	José	Kelly	Leo	Giana	Angie	Derek	Marc	Nicole	Tim	James	Ruth
B.W.	i	ll								ll										
1st	1	l														ll				
2nd		1														ll				
W.up		l														i				
Tot.	8	5		Ab						8						5				
B.W.		ll														ll				
1st		l														l				
2nd								Ill												
W.up								ll												
Tot.		7		Ab				5								8				
B.W.	ll	ll														ll				
1st																l				
2nd																				
W.up																				
Tot.	8	8								Ab						7				
B.W.	1																			
1st																				
2nd	1																			
W.up		l														ll				
Tot.	8	9														8				
B.W.																				
1st																				
2nd		Ill																		
W.up	l	ll																		
Tot.	9	5								l										

WEEK OF 2 / 4 / 13

Notice that the teacher only records tallies for point deductions when a student is off task; hence, the empty spaces are worth the maximum points. For the students who have no tallies, and are present for the day, they each earned 10 points = 100%.

This strategy has also been used for individual students rather than an entire class. The teacher simply arranges with the student a cue of some type, such as a tap on the desk when they are to record the points that they believe they deserve.

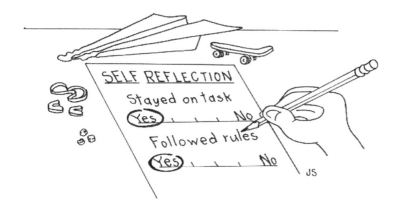

As hard as Mr. Cline tried, he could never
get Dennis to truly self-reflect.

TIP

39

Self-reflection can be
a powerful tool.

"Running the Course"

As hard as teachers try, and as much as they may want a student to improve his behavior, sometimes it just doesn't happen. This is frustrating. What does a teacher do now? Refer back to "The Non-Compliant" (Tip 29). Has everything listed been done? What's left?

- Referrals to counselor and/or administrator <u>written objectively</u>

- School-wide Support Team contacted for suggestions (Most schools have some type of student study team.)

- C.A.R.E. (Child at Risk in Education) referral for possible special education services

As a teacher, there will always be some things that are out of your control. There will be times when a child is simply set on "running the course"—going through all the consequences of their misbehaviors. The key here is to leave no rock unturned and never give up—in other words, stay professional. A good doctor never gives up on his patients—neither should a teacher ever give up on any student. Eventually, the child will appreciate your efforts, even if not during the time you have him in class. Don't be surprised when a child comes back years later to say, "Thank you." <u>You will always be remembered as the one who never gave up</u>.

TIP 40

Leave no rock unturned when a student is set on "Running the Course."

"Positive Talk"

Put yourself into the shoes of a parent who has a disobedient child. Even if the student is only a kindergartener, do you think the parent has already been informed by others, such as the babysitter or child care workers, of the child's misbehaviors? As the years go on, the parent may even become defensive or accusatory—blaming others and/or the "system."

Parents of a seventh grader sat in a conference and said, "Mike was ruined by his second grade teacher, Mrs. _____. Before having her, he loved school and didn't have any problems."

How many conferences deal with a child's misbehavior or poor attitude? Is a teacher obligated to provide the parents with an accurate picture? Will having the parents in your corner, backing you up, be to the child's benefit—not to mention make life easier for you as the teacher?

With the exception of the back to school/introductory conferences and the end-of-the-year, How-did-we-do? conferences, most deal with the 10–20% of students who are non-compliant. Teachers are obligated to provide an accurate academic and behavioral picture of their students. Children will always stand a better chance of improving when the parents and their teachers are "on the same page." And of course, teachers' lives are definitely easier when they have the parents' support.

So what is the answer? There isn't a quick and easy fix. There rarely is, but there is one tip that may help take the parents off the defensive and put them into a supportive role—"Positive Talk." Here is how it works:

1. After introductory remarks, begin phone or face-to-face conferences with a statement of caring that places you on the same side of the parent.

2. If time, ask about the student. Taking an interest is another way to show you care.

3. <u>Tell the parent what the child needs to do</u> rather than what the child is doing wrong. The same message gets across, but there is less sting in the statements. Pretend that you are the parent and read the following:

Non-examples	Examples
Lilly constantly talks and interrupts me during my instruction.	Lilly needs to be a good listener during instruction.
Nick never comes to school with his text and supplies.	Nick needs to check his book bag every night to make sure that he brings his text and supplies to school.
Alex doesn't get along well with her classmates.	Alex needs to develop friendships.

(The second column of statements feels less oppositional but still provides an accurate picture.)

4. Before the conference, write a positive talk script—especially if you have forewarning that the parent has a reputation for being uncooperative.

5. Agree on a follow-up time to have a phone conference. Hopefully, just knowing that there will be another contact will help the child, you, and the parent to stay focused on the child's goals.

6. Never ask a parent to do more than two things at a time. One request is even better.

Teacher side of conference:

I have a concern for Ricky. I want him to be successful and to do the very best that he can.

Do you have time to talk for a few minutes? Could you tell me a little about Ricky? What does he like to do when not in school? Does he participate in any sports, clubs, or hobbies? What are his responsibilities at home: chores, expected behaviors, etc.?

The concern that I have is this: Ricky needs to be a good listener during instruction. He needs to focus on me, wait until I finish my explanation and modeling, and then, raise his hand if he has any questions.

I have a tally card he is using. This will be in his agenda with my signature. Would you be willing to sign it each evening? I'm only asking you to congratulate him when he makes his goal. I'll make it obvious when he does.

Thank you. Can we set up a time for a follow-up phone confer-ence in approximately two weeks? That would be great! Same time? I look forward to talking to you again.

<u>Positive Talk Script</u> (Notes you write <u>before</u> the conference):

I have a concern for Ricky. I want him to be successful and to do the very best that he can.

Do you have time to talk for a few minutes?

Sports, clubs, or hobbies? Responsibilities at home?

Concern: needs to be a good listener during instruction.

Focus, listen, and raise hand for questions

Explain tally card.

Set follow-up phone conference.

Remember that anytime a parent helps, it is a real bonus. As experienced teachers know, there will always be a few parents you will never win over. Just as with the students, however, be the professional and never give up.

TIP 41

Positive talk may help you gain parental support.

Instruction

"Being Well Prepared"

Your lessons must be well prepared for you to give classroom management adequate attention. If you are busy getting materials together, or revising plans up to the last minute, you won't be able to greet your students at the door or have the withitness to be a keen observer during instruction—two fundamentals. Experienced teachers know that there is a positive correlation between being well prepared and having a good day.

Some excellent advice is to never leave your classroom until everything is set for the next day. If you have to leave your classroom early because of coaching, family obligations, etc., then never go to bed until your plans are set for the next day, and if possible, go to work early enough to lay out materials.

All of this comes down to dedication, but it is actually doing yourself a favor. Well-planned days are less stressful.

TIP 42

Being well prepared allows you to focus on managing student behavior.

"Engagement"

Yo ou have heard the phrase: *Idle hands make for mischief.* You could probably stretch that statement to include: *Bored students make for mischief.* Think back about the times that either you or a peer misbehaved in class. Was any of it related to not having anything to do or being bored? Not all lessons are going to spark the interest of all students, but there are a few things you can do to raise your students' engagement.

Your voice was mentioned earlier regarding your presence. Monotones put people to sleep. Varying your pitch and volume raises engagement. Be expressive with both your voice and movements.

Use your proximity. Not only does being near your students reduce misbehaviors, but it also improves their engagement. As recommended previously, teach among your students. Move around whenever your lesson doesn't require you to be at the board or any electronics.

Here are just a few more suggestions:

1. <u>Sell your lesson</u>. Motivate your learners with your enthusiasm and a hook—something to give relevance or interest like a real world connection, video clip, or artifact.

2. <u>Include students' names in your explanations</u>. Example: *Elizabeth, you are the president of Country A, and you*

desperately need petroleum. Derek, you rule Country B and have plenty of it. The problem is Derek's country is an enemy of Elizabeth's closest ally, Country C. Cindy, the queen of Country C, is asking all countries to support her trade embargo against Country B. What should Elizabeth do? This strategy pulls students into the lesson.

3. <u>Do frequent comprehension checks</u>. Students are more attentive if they are held accountable.

    - Random questioning
    - Quick quizzes
    - Individual whiteboards, which render 100% participation (Carefully plan your procedures for both the materials and their use.)
    - ActiVotes or ActivExpressions, which also include the whole class

(Whenever comprehension checks reveal that students are not understanding the lesson, reteach to individuals or small groups.)

4. <u>Use "change of state."</u> Remember that students' attention spans are roughly equivalent to their ages. Teach with variety. Use graphic organizers, foldables (creative ways to fold paper into graphic organizers), projects, technology, academic games, drawings, diagrams, magazines, jigsawing (breaking content apart for different teams who report back to class), etc.

    - Provide students opportunities to discuss and share their ideas and knowledge. Use Kagan cooperative learning structures. If you're not familiar with these, take a workshop. It will raise your student engagement immediately.

- Chunk your instruction and do a processing activity after each piece.

5. Challenge your students by promoting high order thinking skills (H.O.T.S.) Use fewer verbs like: list, define, describe and identify, and more like: demonstrate, compare, create, and summarize.

6. Prepare sponge activities for those who complete their work early. You could even print a poster of options, such as:

- Read your chapter book.
- Work on an approved computer program.
- Use class notes to write test questions.
- Quiz a study buddy using flash cards or notes.
- Write a paragraph using as many of the current vocabulary words as possible.
- Complete bonus work.
- Etc.

Anything that is relevant to your curriculum is a potential sponge activity. Giving value to this work is always helpful, especially for middle and high school students.

7. Offer an occasional choice of topics or activities. It raises interest. This is particularly true for projects.

TIP

43 Keep your students engaged.

"Clarity"

If you were a student, which would you rather be known as: a dummy or a trouble maker? That's not much of a choice, is it?

All misbehaviors have a cause. Sometimes the source is poor reading, writing, or problem-solving skills.

Clarity of instruction and directions can diminish some of the misbehaviors caused by students trying to avoid the appearance of being dumb.

Try these strategies:

- Begin every lesson by stating a clear, student-friendly objective. Post it in the same place every day.

- Whenever there are multiple instructions or steps, clearly print or draw them. This will assist those students who occasionally "tune out." (It will also save you time by not having to repeat them.)

- Whenever you teach a lesson that has a procedure or steps, try the following in order:

  1. Explain the procedure/steps

  2. Model the "How to" using metacognition—think aloud.

  3. Model the "How to" again by having students tell you what to write and why. You be the scribe.

4. <u>Provide the students with risk-free practice</u>. Having them do this in pairs or in teams of three with students alternating or rotating steps works well. The students will assist one another. You can walk around during this time, monitor, and reteach.

5. <u>Provide individual practice time</u>.

6. Pull out students who are still struggling and <u>do small group instruction</u>.

- <u>Pair up students heterogeneously</u> for study buddies.

- <u>Post homework in the same place every day</u>.

- <u>Provide experiential background</u> when needed:
  □ Reveal key vocabulary before a reading.
  □ Review prerequisites before moving on.
  □ Provide a picture, an example, or a non-example so a relationship can be formed.

- <u>Give think time</u> before calling for an answer and coach when needed.

- <u>Many students' learning styles require visuals</u>. Printing or drawing things makes a difference for these learners.

All of these strategies are also ways to show students you care.

TIP 44 Clarity of instruction and directions will improve student behavior.

Summary

What defines great teachers? They...

- Have the capacity to care about their students and the ability to let it show.
- Establish procedures that become routines.
- Have the presence that attracts students' attention.
- Are professional in both appearance and actions.
- Have keen withitness to see all and hear all.
- Create the best possible seating assignments.
- Use immediate, subtle redirections to keep minor misbehaviors from snowballing.
- Follow up on all redirections to ensure compliance.
- Create solid, comfortable behavior plans with expectations, consequences, and rewards.
- Use their behavior plans with consistency.
- Have patience with the "non-compliant" and the fortitude to never give up on them.

- Privately conference with students without "backing them into corners."
- Keep their composure during challenging times.
- Take pride in their instruction.
- Maintain high levels of student engagement.
- Deliver instruction with clarity.

Every teacher has a few bad days. The difference between a poor teacher and a great teacher is that the poor teacher complains while the great teacher regroups and rallies.

Good Luck!
Jim Shaulis

References

1. Boynton, M. & Boynton, C. (2005). *Preventing and Solving Discipline Problems*. Alexandria, VA: ASCD.

2. Clark, R. (2004). *The Excellent 11*. New York, NY: Hyperion.

3. Jones, F. H. with Jones, P. & Jones, J. (2007). *Tools for Teaching*. Santa Cruz, CA: Fredric H. Jones & Associates.

4. Jones, J. L. & Carpenter, L. (Producers) & Jones, F. (Director). (2007). *Tool for Teaching Video Toolbox* [Video series, Disc 9/10, "Eliminating Backtalk"]. Phoenix, AZ.

5. Kagan, S., Kyle, P. & Scott, S. (2004). *Win-Win Discipline*. San Clemente, CA: Kagan.

6. Marzano, R. J. with Marzano, J. S. & Pickering, D.J. (2003). *Classroom Management That Works*. Alexandra, VA: ASCD.

7. Payne, R. K. (2005). *A Framework for Understanding Poverty*. Highlands, TX: aha! Process.

8. Payne, R. K. (Author/Director). (2005). *A Framework for Understanding Poverty*, [DVD series, Module 6, "Discipline Interventions"]. Highlands, TX: aha! Process.

9. Stipek, D. (2006, Sept.). Relationships Matter. *Educational Leadership* 64(1), 46-49.

10. Wong, H. K. & Wong, R.T. (2009). *The First Days of School.* Singapore, CS Graphics Pte. Ltd.

11. 42 years experience in education

About the Author

Jim Shaulis has worked in public education for 42 years—30 as a classroom teacher. He has taught a variety of subjects at three different levels: elementary, secondary, and college (part-time instructor at Illinois State University).

He has been an assistant principal of a middle school and a principal of a K-8 school. Administration went well, but his love was always teaching.

During his last nine years, Jim observed, coached, and taught elementary and secondary teachers while working in Professional Development for the Sarasota County School District in Sarasota, Florida.

Some of his honors:

- Sarasota Middle School Teacher of the Year 1989–1990
- Sarasota County Middle School Teacher of the Year 1995–1996
- Sarasota County Inclusion Teacher of the Year 1999–2000

Has conducted many workshops: Classroom Management, Learning Strategies, Student Engagement, Parent-Teacher Conferencing, Homework & Study Skills for Parents, and others.

His hope is that his years of experience will benefit today's educators.

CPSIA information can be obtained at www.ICGtesting.com
Printed in the USA
BVOW021315110613

323022BV00003B/6/P